Book

Specific Skill Series

Working Within Words

Richard A. Boning

Fifth Edition

D1537654

SRA/McGraw-Hill
Columbus, Ohio

Cover, Back Cover, Ron Sanford/The Stock Market

SRA/McGraw-Hill

A Division of The **McGraw·Hill** *Companies*

Printed in the United States of America.

Send all inquiries to:
    SRA/McGraw-Hill
    250 Old Wilson Bridge Road, Suite 310
    Worthington, OH 43085

ISBN 0-02-687924-7

    5 6 7 8 9 IMP 00 99

To the Teacher

PURPOSE:
WORKING WITHIN WORDS helps pupils put sounds and other word elements to work to determine word meaning. Many units in WORKING WITHIN WORDS develop understandings about sound-symbol (phonic) associations. Other units treat letter combinations, syllabication, roots and affixes, accent patterns, compound words, longer words, and spelling changes caused by adding endings.

FOR WHOM:
The skill of WORKING WITHIN WORDS is developed through a series of books spanning ten levels (Picture, Preparatory, A, B, C, D, E, F, G, H). The Picture Level is for pupils who have not acquired a basic sight vocabulary. The Preparatory Level is for pupils who have a basic sight vocabulary but are not yet ready for the first-grade-level book. Books A through H are appropriate for pupils who can read on levels one through eight, respectively. **The use of the *Specific Skill Series Placement Test* is recommended to determine the appropriate level.**

THE NEW EDITION:
The fifth edition of the *Specific Skill Series* maintains the quality and focus that has distinguished this program for more than 25 years. A key element central to the program's success has been the unique nature of the reading selections. Nonfiction pieces about current topics have been designed to stimulate the interest of students, motivating them to use the comprehension strategies they have learned to further their reading. To keep this important aspect of the program intact, a percentage of the reading selections have been replaced in order to ensure the continued relevance of the subject material.

In addition, a significant percentage of the artwork in the program has been replaced to give the books a contemporary look. The cover photographs are designed to appeal to readers of all ages.

SESSIONS:
Short practice sessions are the most effective. It is desirable to have a practice session every day or every other day, using a few units each session.

SCORING:
Pupils should record their answers on the reproducible worksheets. The worksheets make scoring easier and provide uniform records of the pupils' work. Using worksheets also avoids consuming the exercise books.

It is important for pupils to know how well they are doing. For this reason, units should be scored as soon as they have been completed. Then a discussion can be held in which pupils justify their choices. (The Integrated Language Activities, many of which are open-ended, do not lend themselves to an objective score; thus there are no answer keys for these pages.)

GENERAL INFORMATION ON *WORKING WITHIN WORDS*:

The units are of two types: concept builders and functional exercises. The concept units focus the reader's attention on common patterns and parts of words. Each generalization is built step-by-step on the structure of previously formed concepts. The functional exercises either follow the concept units or are contained within them. They provide the reader with many immediate and repeated experiences with words involving particular patterns or principles. Sentence settings are typical for the pupils' level; often the choices offered are new words.

As WORKING WITHIN WORDS progresses through different word elements there is constant reinforcement. The more elementary booklets focus on phonic elements such as consonant sounds, consonant substitutions, blends, phonograms, and vowel sounds. As the level of difficulty increases, the emphasis shifts to syllabication, prefixes, suffixes, and roots.

A unit-by-unit list of concepts developed in this book is found on page 64.

INSTRUCTIONS:

Minimal direction is required. Pupils' attention must be drawn to the answer choices. In the concept units only two or three answer choices are offered. In the units that provide application of understandings, four to nine answer choices are offered, providing more experiences with words of a particular pattern. In units which offer an *F* choice, the *F* stands for NONE. This means that none of the choices makes sense in that particular setting.

RELATED MATERIALS:

Specific Skill Series Placement Tests, which enable the teacher to place pupils at their appropriate levels in each skill, are available for the Elementary (Pre-1–6) and Midway (4–8) grade levels.

About This Book

In written words, letters stand for sounds. A reader **decodes** a word the way a spy decodes a secret message. If you know the sounds that letters stand for, you can begin to unlock the secret message of a word.

Knowing the sounds of a word is only a beginning. Just as a secret message may have many parts, a word may have more than one part, too. In order to read and understand a word, you need to understand the parts of the word.

Words can be divided into **syllables**. A syllable is a word part that contains a **vowel sound**. The word *dog* has just one vowel sound. It is a one-syllable word. The word *rocket* has two vowel sounds. It is a two-syllable word. How many syllables does the word *syllable* have?

Word parts can be added to words to create new words with new meanings. For example, you may *like* most fruits but *dislike* lemons. How did the word part *dis* change the meaning of the word *like*?

In this book, you will study many words. You will learn to recognize the parts of words and patterns in words. Then you will use what you have learned. As you unlock the meanings of the words in this book, you will be practicing the skills of a master decoder!

1. The twenty-six letters in the alphabet are divided into _____ groups known as vowels and consonants.

   (A) two   **(B) three**   **(C) four**

2. The letters **a, e, i, o, u** (and sometimes **y**) are called vowels. There are five vowels not counting the letter **y**. The other letters are called _____.

   (A) syllables   **(B) long sounds**   **(C) consonants**

3. Each of the vowels has _____ main sounds. They are called long and short vowel sounds.

   (A) two   **(B) three**   **(C) four**

4. In some words, such as **hi, go, she,** the vowel comes at the _____ and says its own name.

   (A) middle   **(B) end**   **(C) start**

5. When vowels say their own _____ we call them long vowel sounds.

   (A) consonants   **(B) short sounds**   **(C) names**

6. In such words as **smack, drip, trust** there is only one vowel and that vowel is in the _____ of the word.

   (A) beginning   **(B) middle**   **(C) front**

7. When there is only one vowel and that vowel is in the middle of the word, the vowel usually has a _____ sound.

   (A) long   **(B) short**   **(C) ringing**

8. The position of the single vowel in a word gives the reader a _____ idea as to its sound.

   (A) poor   **(B) new**   **(C) good**

9. When the only vowel in a word is at the end (as in the word **he**) that vowel usually has a long _____.

   (A) sound   **(B) syllable**   **(C) consonant**

10. When the only vowel in a word is found in the middle of the word, it usually has a _____ sound.

    (A) silent   **(B) long**   **(C) short**

UNIT 2
Building Vowel Concepts

1. Listen to the vowel sound in the words **glide, scene, bone, snake, cute.** The first vowel in each of these words says its own _____.
   (A) **name**   (B) **number**   (C) **color**

2. Words that have an **e** at the end are often called **Magic E** words. The **e** makes the _____ that comes before it say its own name.
   (A) **consonant**   (B) **vowel**   (C) **line**

3. Look at the words **hope** and **hoping.** The letter **e** at the end of the word **hope** is _____ before the ending **ing** is added.
   (A) **doubled**   (B) **dropped**   (C) **silent**

4. The letter **o** in the word **hoping** says its own name. The first vowels in the words **taking, poking, hiding** also say their own names even though the _____ has been dropped.
   (A) **i**   (B) **a**   (C) **e**

5. Words such as **hoping** and **taking** were **Magic E** words before the endings were added. They still keep the _____ vowel sound.
   (A) **short**   (B) **long**   (C) **silent**

6. Listen to the vowel sound in the words **steam, chain, creep, float.** In each word the first vowel says its own name while the _____ vowel is silent.
   (A) **third**   (B) **second**   (C) **first**

7. In most **Double Vowel** words that have an **oa, ea, ee,** or **ai,** the first vowel says its own name and the _____ vowel is silent.
   (A) **second**   (B) **third**   (C) **tenth**

8. There are some words such as **bread, dead** in which the first vowel is not long even though there are _____ vowels together.
   (A) **one**   (B) **two**   (C) **three**

9. There are other **Double Vowel** words such as the **ie** words (**belief, chief, thief**) in which the second _____ is heard.
   (A) **vowel**   (B) **consonant**   (C) **number**

10. If you meet a **Double Vowel** word that you don't know, give the first vowel a long sound. If the word still doesn't make sense, you must be willing to _____ the vowel sound.
    (A) **keep**   (B) **change**   (C) **hide**

1. Listen for the sound of the **y** as you say the words **cry, try, sly.** The **y** at the end of these words sounds like a long _____.

   (A) o   (B) i   (C) e

2. Listen for the sound of the **y** as you say the words **easy, sleepy, happy.** The letter **y** at the end of these words sounds like a long _____.

   (A) a   (B) o   (C) e

3. Listen for the sound of the **y** as you say the word **gym.** The **y** in the middle of this word has a _____ **i** sound.

   (A) long   (B) short   (C) silent

4. Listen for the short **i** sound the _____ makes in the first syllable of the word **sympathy.**

   (A) y   (B) x   (C) e

5. In the word **dry** the **y** has a long **i** sound. In the word **happily** the **y** has a long **e** sound. In the word **myth** the _____ has a short **i** sound.

   (A) y   (B) t   (C) e

6. In the word **bakery** the **y** has a long **e** sound. In the word **memory** the **y** has a long **e** sound. The **y** in the word **cry** has a _____ **i** sound.

   (A) long   (B) short   (C) silent

7. The **y** in the word **crazy** has a long **e** sound. The **y** in the word **pony** has a long _____ sound.

   (A) e   (B) i   (C) a

8. Listen to the sound of each of the vowels as you say the words **star, her, bird, corn, turn.** In these words the _____ have no long or short sounds.

   (A) consonants   (B) vowels   (C) r's

9. Look at the words **star, her, bird, corn, turn.** Notice the letter that comes after the vowel. In each word it is an _____.

   (A) r   (B) x   (C) i

10. When the letter **r** comes after a vowel, the vowel is neither long nor _____.

    (A) magic   (B) short   (C) sounded

1. The **gl**_____**w** of the fire could be seen from far away.
   - (A) long o
   - (B) short e
   - (C) short u
   - (D) short i
   - (E) short o
   - (F) NONE

2. Kelly saw me **c**_____**tch** the ball.
   - (A) short u
   - (B) long u
   - (C) short a
   - (D) short i
   - (E) long a
   - (F) NONE

3. I have to **st**_____**p** at the library after school.
   - (A) long e
   - (B) long i
   - (C) short o
   - (D) long a
   - (E) long u
   - (F) NONE

4. Tom got a new book **b**_____**g** for his birthday.
   - (A) long o
   - (B) short o
   - (C) short a
   - (D) short i
   - (E) long a
   - (F) NONE

5. Pick up your toys or someone will **st**_____**mble.**
   - (A) long a
   - (B) short e
   - (C) short i
   - (D) short u
   - (E) short o
   - (F) NONE

6. Jill ate a **sl**_____**ce** of cake.
   - (A) long o
   - (B) short a
   - (C) long e
   - (D) long i
   - (E) short u
   - (F) NONE

7. Please teach Peter how to **sk**_____**p.**
   - (A) long e
   - (B) short e
   - (C) short a
   - (D) short u
   - (E) long u
   - (F) NONE

8. Mother reminded us not to **sl**_____**m** the door.
   - (A) long i
   - (B) short i
   - (C) long o
   - (D) long u
   - (E) short u
   - (F) NONE

9. We could not open the window because it was **st**_____**ck.**
   - (A) short i
   - (B) long u
   - (C) short u
   - (D) long a
   - (E) short o
   - (F) NONE

10. Can you **sp**_____**ll** every word on the list?
    - (A) long i
    - (B) long u
    - (C) long e
    - (D) long o
    - (E) short i
    - (F) NONE

1. I know we can **tr**_____**st** Jan to complete the job.
   - **(A) long i**
   - **(B) short i**
   - **(C) short u**
   - **(D) short o**
   - **(E) long a**
   - **(F) NONE**

2. Ron could not find a **tr**_____**ce** of our missing cat.
   - **(A) long e**
   - **(B) long a**
   - **(C) short u**
   - **(D) short e**
   - **(E) long o**
   - **(F) NONE**

3. We **m**_____**st** do our homework now.
   - **(A) long i**
   - **(B) short e**
   - **(C) short u**
   - **(D) short o**
   - **(E) short i**
   - **(F) NONE**

4. Andy **cl**_____**pped** for the winning team.
   - **(A) long e**
   - **(B) short a**
   - **(C) long a**
   - **(D) short i**
   - **(E) long u**
   - **(F) NONE**

5. That oil truck is **h**_____**ge**.
   - **(A) long i**
   - **(B) short o**
   - **(C) long a**
   - **(D) short e**
   - **(E) long u**
   - **(F) NONE**

6. Donna said that she could **sw**_____**m** the length of the pool.
   - **(A) long e**
   - **(B) long u**
   - **(C) short i**
   - **(D) long i**
   - **(E) short e**
   - **(F) NONE**

7. It is not **w**_____**se** to cross the street without looking.
   - **(A) short e**
   - **(B) short u**
   - **(C) long a**
   - **(D) long i**
   - **(E) long e**
   - **(F) NONE**

8. Maria told a **j**_____**ke** that made the whole class laugh.
   - **(A) long a**
   - **(B) long e**
   - **(C) long u**
   - **(D) long i**
   - **(E) short a**
   - **(F) NONE**

9. How many people can play this **g**_____**me**?
   - **(A) short i**
   - **(B) long i**
   - **(C) short a**
   - **(D) short e**
   - **(E) long e**
   - **(F) NONE**

10. We **sp**_____**nt** all of our money on the present.
    - **(A) long i**
    - **(B) short i**
    - **(C) short a**
    - **(D) short e**
    - **(E) long u**
    - **(F) NONE**

1. She can draw a straight **l_____ne** with the ruler.
(A) long u	(B) short i	(C) short e
(D) long a	(E) short a	(F) NONE

2. I am sure I **f_____lt** a raindrop on my head.
(A) short e	(B) long e	(C) long i
(D) short i	(E) short o	(F) NONE

3. The number that comes between eight and ten is **n_____ne.**
(A) long o	(B) short a	(C) long a
(D) long i	(E) short i	(F) NONE

4. What do they sell in this **sh_____p?**
(A) short u	(B) long u	(C) short e
(D) long o	(E) long e	(F) NONE

5. Alice found a pretty **sh_____ll** at the seashore.
(A) short i	(B) long o	(C) short a
(D) short e	(E) long i	(F) NONE

6. My kitten will **l_____ck** the milk from the plate.
(A) short e	(B) short i	(C) long u
(D) long a	(E) short a	(F) NONE

7. There was a snow **dr_____ft** seven feet high.
(A) long i	(B) short u	(C) long e
(D) short i	(E) long a	(F) NONE

8. We walked **p_____st** Mark's house to the corner.
(A) short e	(B) long i	(C) short i
(D) long o	(E) short u	(F) NONE

9. There is nothing quite like a cool **dr_____nk** of water.
(A) short e	(B) long u	(C) short u
(D) short i	(E) long o	(F) NONE

10. The snow did not **m_____lt** until spring.
(A) short i	(B) short o	(C) short e
(D) long a	(E) short u	(F) NONE

1. We looked at all the new cars in the _____.
   - (A) showroom
   - (B) warpath
   - (C) anybody
   - (D) headlight
   - (E) sunstroke
   - (F) NONE

2. A dark _____ casts its shadow on the ground.
   - (A) underline
   - (B) southwest
   - (C) thundercloud
   - (D) wholesale
   - (E) anyone
   - (F) NONE

3. The friendly _____ served our family a tasty meal.
   - (A) sunstroke
   - (B) innkeeper
   - (C) toothpick
   - (D) wayside
   - (E) viewpoint
   - (F) NONE

4. When did you lose your _____?
   - (A) everywhere
   - (B) watertight
   - (C) warehouse
   - (D) streamline
   - (E) pocketbook
   - (F) NONE

5. The teacher asked us to copy the story from the _____.
   - (A) springboard
   - (B) sailboat
   - (C) whenever
   - (D) shoelace
   - (E) chalkboard
   - (F) NONE

6. What should I write on this _____?
   - (A) earring
   - (B) overcoat
   - (C) iceberg
   - (D) postcard
   - (E) watchtower
   - (F) NONE

7. Aunt Bess caught a 200-pound _____ on her line.
   - (A) rainfall
   - (B) housework
   - (C) swordfish
   - (D) hereafter
   - (E) safekeeping
   - (F) NONE

8. He replied, "You will have to look _____ for the gift."
   - (A) streetcar
   - (B) elsewhere
   - (C) anyone
   - (D) shipyard
   - (E) anything
   - (F) NONE

9. We heard the booming sound of thunder _____ the night.
   - (A) whirlwind
   - (B) snowstorm
   - (C) whenever
   - (D) wherever
   - (E) farmyard
   - (F) NONE

10. We should be traveling north on this _____.
    - (A) highway
    - (B) person
    - (C) headlights
    - (D) outcry
    - (E) carfare
    - (F) NONE

1. I was _____ because I had lost my ring.

   (A) seacoast   (B) headset   (C) broadcast
   (D) battlefield   (E) upset   (F) NONE

2. The tall _____ on the ship reached high into the sky.

   (A) shipwreck   (B) seacoast   (C) raincoat
   (D) smokestack   (E) bedtime   (F) NONE

3. We could cross the river only when the _____ came down.

   (A) footstep   (B) warpath   (C) rainstorm
   (D) snowball   (E) drawbridge   (F) NONE

4. The searchlight from the _____ could be seen far away.

   (A) moonlight   (B) sunrise   (C) housework
   (D) lighthouse   (E) candlelight   (F) NONE

5. Are you sure our tent is _____?

   (A) schoolyard   (B) something   (C) touchdown
   (D) anyhow   (E) waterproof   (F) NONE

6. From the _____ we could see the trees many miles away.

   (A) throughout   (B) wintertime   (C) overboard
   (D) homesick   (E) sometime   (F) NONE

7. It is pleasant to hear the chirp of a _____.

   (A) wildcat   (B) footstep   (C) airplane
   (D) bullfight   (E) songbird   (F) NONE

8. I will need a _____ to reach that shelf.

   (A) woodlands   (B) cowgirl   (C) workrooms
   (D) stepladder   (E) basketballs   (F) NONE

9. I had _____ for breakfast this morning.

   (A) oatmeal   (B) telltale   (C) lonesome
   (D) goldfish   (E) fishhook   (F) NONE

10. We gave the _____ when we entered the clubhouse.

    (A) household   (B) beanstalk   (C) hallway
    (D) hilltop   (E) password   (F) NONE

1. Is it easy for the acrobat to walk on a _____?

    (A) skyline   (B) seagoing   (C) topsail
    (D) headlight   (E) tightrope   (F) NONE

2. I couldn't see the words on the _____ because of the fog.

    (A) weekend   (B) alongside   (C) shopkeeper
    (D) signpost   (E) searchlight   (F) NONE

3. What is in the _____ of that painting?

    (A) overturn   (B) background   (C) leftover
    (D) homework   (E) outspread   (F) NONE

4. Wash that _____ off the glass.

    (A) teamwork   (B) highland   (C) fingerprint
    (D) wrongdoing   (E) inside   (F) NONE

5. We went on a _____ tour as soon as we arrived in town.

    (A) standstill   (B) cardboard   (C) lifetime
    (D) fireside   (E) sightseeing   (F) NONE

6. He is _____ because he eats too much.

    (A) overlook   (B) headache   (C) overweight
    (D) overhead   (E) sometime   (F) NONE

7. The _____ floated over the sides of the washbasin.

    (A) seaside   (B) watertight   (C) seacoast
    (D) soapsuds   (E) highway   (F) NONE

8. Mother bought the medicine at the _____.

    (A) hillside   (B) eyelids   (C) sunbeam
    (D) spotlight   (E) drugstore   (F) NONE

9. It was beautiful to watch the _____ from the mountaintop.

    (A) footstep   (B) homemade   (C) sunrise
    (D) armchair   (E) somewhere   (F) NONE

10. The lady put the money into the _____.

    (A) weekday   (B) strongbox   (C) sandstorm
    (D) sickbed   (E) yardstick   (F) NONE

1. The letters **aw** and **au** often make the same sound. The **aw** in the word **jaw** sounds like the _____ in the word **taught.**

    (A) au   (B) gh   (C) ht

2. We set off on the trip at _____.

    (A) sprawl   (B) dawn   (C) audience
    (D) faucet   (E) awful   (F) NONE

3. There was fresh _____ in the barn.

    (A) crawl   (B) fault   (C) haul
    (D) straw   (E) pour   (F) NONE

4. Jack and Peggy were in the yard hanging up the _____.

    (A) autumn   (B) automobile   (C) yawn
    (D) Paul   (E) claw   (F) NONE

5. Please pour the _____ on the meat.

    (A) sauce   (B) awnings   (C) laundry
    (D) sausage   (E) brought   (F) NONE

6. The letters **ew** and **oo** often make the same sound. The **ew** in the word **grew** sounds almost like the _____ in the word **moon.**

    (A) mo   (B) oo   (C) on

7. I didn't know it was _____ until he took off the mask.

    (A) chew   (B) troop   (C) broom
    (D) stool   (E) Lewis   (F) NONE

8. A few more days like this and the flowers will _____.

    (A) smooth   (B) balloon   (C) bloom
    (D) drew   (E) blew   (F) NONE

9. My Aunt Matilda made some tasty _____ for dinner.

    (A) choose   (B) loose   (C) grew
    (D) baboon   (E) stew   (F) NONE

10. We thought that he did it, but we didn't have _____.

    (A) threw   (B) spoon   (C) flew
    (D) crew   (E) proof   (F) NONE

1. The letters **ou** and **ow** often make the same sound. The **ou** in the word **house** sounds like the _____ in the word **crowd.**

   (A) win   (B) nd   (C) ow

2. They put the _____ on top of the queen's head.

   (A) **thousand**   (B) **crown**   (C) **crowd**
   (D) **cloud**   (E) **found**   (F) **NONE**

3. Don't talk when your _____ is full of food!

   (A) **drown**   (B) **mouth**   (C) **scout**
   (D) **shower**   (E) **shout**   (F) **NONE**

4. We just heard them _____ the weather over the radio.

   (A) **doubt**   (B) **powder**   (C) **announce**
   (D) **chowder**   (E) **tower**   (F) **NONE**

5. Cindy spilled milk on her new _____ and skirt.

   (A) **ounce**   (B) **blouse**   (C) **vowel**
   (D) **clown**   (E) **ground**   (F) **NONE**

6. What was the _____ of the bill?

   (A) **hound**   (B) **towel**   (C) **amount**
   (D) **growl**   (E) **crouch**   (F) **NONE**

7. Mother said that it was a long walk to the top of the _____.

   (A) **gown**   (B) **drown**   (C) **flour**
   (D) **hound**   (E) **pounded**   (F) **NONE**

8. The letters **oi** and **oy** make the same sound. The **oi** in the word **join** sounds like the **oy** in the word _____.

   (A) **joy**   (B) **automobile**   (C) **saying**

9. Please don't _____ me when I am studying.

   (A) **poison**   (B) **boil**   (C) **broil**
   (D) **annoy**   (E) **choice**   (F) **NONE**

10. The cake was _____ and delicious.

    (A) **coin**   (B) **destroy**   (C) **voice**
    (D) **moist**   (E) **joyful**   (F) **NONE**

1. It is _____ that you listen very carefully.
   - (A) starve
   - (B) harmless
   - (C) remark
   - (D) important
   - (E) porter
   - (F) NONE

2. It was difficult to hit the _____ from that distance.
   - (A) target
   - (B) history
   - (C) torture
   - (D) hardly
   - (E) artistic
   - (F) NONE

3. Rita read an interesting _____ from the newspaper.
   - (A) charcoal
   - (B) afford
   - (C) harmony
   - (D) article
   - (E) border
   - (F) NONE

4. _____ to the plans we should arrive there soon.
   - (A) Memory
   - (B) According
   - (C) Garlic
   - (D) Torches
   - (E) Store
   - (F) NONE

5. We will go to the _____ to buy fruit.
   - (A) sport
   - (B) carpenter
   - (C) regard
   - (D) barnacle
   - (E) market
   - (F) NONE

6. Paul was very _____ about his clothes and belongings.
   - (A) support
   - (B) cornet
   - (C) armor
   - (D) particular
   - (E) sport
   - (F) NONE

7. The people enjoyed Jean's outstanding _____ very much.
   - (A) hornet
   - (B) marble
   - (C) harvest
   - (D) ignorant
   - (E) performance
   - (F) NONE

8. Juan and his sister did not go out in the _____.
   - (A) storm
   - (B) scarlet
   - (C) scar
   - (D) opportunity
   - (E) short
   - (F) NONE

9. Our team did not _____ during the game.
   - (A) pardon
   - (B) north
   - (C) score
   - (D) reporter
   - (E) market
   - (F) NONE

10. Danny slowed down as he neared the _____ curve.
    - (A) comfort
    - (B) partner
    - (C) sharp
    - (D) cornstarch
    - (E) party
    - (F) NONE

Every word has at least one vowel sound. Sometimes the vowel sound is long, as in the words *make* and *hope*. Sometimes the vowel sound is short, as in *step* and *sit*. Sometimes two letters together make one vowel sound, as in *sound* and *growl*.

A. Exercising Your Skill

What makes words rhyme? Do the words *make* and *take* rhyme? Look at them. Say them softly to yourself. What is alike about them? Do they begin with the same sound? Are their vowel sounds the same? Do they end with similar sounds? Do the things that are alike about them make them rhyme?

Make and *take* both have the same vowel sound. They also end with the same sound. Because their vowel sounds and endings are the same, *make* and *take* rhyme. Read the words in the box. Then copy the words below the box at the top of a sheet of paper. Under each word on your paper, write the words from the box that rhyme with that word. Can you add more words that rhyme to each list?

base	found	new	taste
clop	few	round	town
boot	hop	stop	trace

face	drop	sound	stew
_____	_____	_____	_____
_____	_____	_____	_____
_____	_____	_____	_____
_____	_____	_____	_____

B. Expanding Your Skill

Compare your lists with the lists your classmates made. Did any of the rhyming words surprise you? With your classmates, take turns suggesting other groups of words that rhyme. Name a word, and have the others each say a word that rhymes with your word.

C. Exploring Language

The Forgetful Writers Club got started on their joke book but didn't quite get it completed. They didn't do the answer key for their riddle page. The task is up to you, the Thought-full Editor. Write each riddle. Finish it with a rhyming pair of words. (You and your classmates may brainstorm together.) The first one is done for you.

> A chicken yard is a __hen__ __pen__ .
> A boat cruise is a _____ _____ .
> To eat at noon is to _____ _____ .
> An insect greeting is a _____ _____ .
> A vacation at the beach is _____ _____ .
> A brush closet is a small _____ _____ .
> A "Ten Cents for a Minute" telephone call is _____ _____ .

After you have finished your answer key, turn this page upside down to check the answers.

Answers: ship trip, munch lunch, bug hug, sun fun, broom room, dime time

D. Expressing Yourself

Choose one of these activities.

1. Try your hand at writing your own jokes with rhyming endings. They can be any form you want. Write questions and make up rhyming answers. Write unfinished statements, like the ones in Part C. Or write the rhyming pairs and have your classmates make up the statements!

2. Not all poems rhyme, but many do. When they do, it's often the last word of every line or every other line that rhymes. Write a rhyming poem. If it seems hard to get started, try beginning with these lines:

> One day while I was taking a walk,
> I met a strange creature; we started to talk.
> It had purple eyes and a shiny green face,
> (You fill in a few more lines.)

1. The furniture in the room was _____.
   - (A) nerve
   - (B) derby
   - (C) modern
   - (D) disturb
   - (E) nurse
   - (F) NONE

2. If we don't fix the _____, we will get no heat.
   - (A) turpentine
   - (B) furnace
   - (C) perfume
   - (D) curve
   - (E) girder
   - (F) NONE

3. Ron was _____ when he got up to speak.
   - (A) serve
   - (B) curtsy
   - (C) shirt
   - (D) mermaid
   - (E) nervous
   - (F) NONE

4. We were in a _____ position to take some pictures.
   - (A) perfect
   - (B) turnip
   - (C) burnt
   - (D) current
   - (E) furnish
   - (F) NONE

5. I would like a _____ for lunch.
   - (A) termite
   - (B) customer
   - (C) pattern
   - (D) hamburger
   - (E) murder
   - (F) NONE

6. The waiter will _____ you next.
   - (A) different
   - (B) hermit
   - (C) serve
   - (D) whirl
   - (E) curtain
   - (F) NONE

7. There are _____ pennies in this purse.
   - (A) further
   - (B) thirty
   - (C) curly
   - (D) furniture
   - (E) firm
   - (F) NONE

8. Be careful when you step off this _____.
   - (A) entertained
   - (B) curb
   - (C) nerve
   - (D) chirped
   - (E) expert
   - (F) NONE

9. Listen to the birds' _____.
   - (A) yesterday
   - (B) buzzer
   - (C) chirping
   - (D) surrender
   - (E) verse
   - (F) NONE

10. What do you feed your pet _____?
    - (A) supervise
    - (B) turtle
    - (C) purse
    - (D) advertise
    - (E) purpose
    - (F) NONE

UNIT 14
Plural Concepts

1. **Plural** means **more than one**. The plural of girl is girls. The plural of boy is boys. To make a word plural we often add an _____.
   (A) r   (B) s   (C) b

2. The plural of some words is made by adding an **es**. Be sure the root word ends with an **x, s, sh, ch** before you add an _____.
   (A) es   (B) m   (C) t

3. The plural of bo**x** is bo**xes**. The plural of bus is bu**ses**. Words that end with an **x** or _____ form their plural by adding an **es**.
   (A) g   (B) s   (C) w

4. The plural of bu**sh** is bu**shes**. The plural of lunch is lun**ches**. Words that end with _____ or **ch** form their plural by adding an **es**.
   (A) m   (B) ph   (C) sh

5. You can remember the letters **x, s, sh, ch** because all of them make the sound a _____ does when it is stopping or starting.
   (A) camel   (B) boat   (C) train

6. Some words end with the letter **f** or **fe** such as half and _____. To make the plural of these words you change **f** or **fe** to **v** and then add **es**.
   (A) lump   (B) life   (C) left

7. The plural of wol**f** is wol**ves**. The plural of wi**fe** is _____.
   (A) wifes   (B) wives   (C) wifs

8. The plural of hal**f** is hal**ves**. The plural of kni**fe** is _____.
   (A) knips   (B) knifs   (C) knives

9. Before you make the plural of words you must find out how the word _____. If the word ends with **x, s, sh,** or **ch,** an **es** is added.
   (A) sees   (B) ends   (C) starts

10. If a word ends with **f** or **fe,** the **f** or **fe** is changed to the letter _____ and an **es** is added.
    (A) b   (B) t   (C) v

1. It was easy to _____ the wood with the ax.
   - (A) splint
   - (B) splendid
   - (C) splatter
   - (D) split
   - (E) splash
   - (F) NONE

2. Did you throw away that _____ of paper?
   - (A) scrap
   - (B) scream
   - (C) knob
   - (D) screech
   - (E) twig
   - (F) NONE

3. The poor animal was _____ by a car.
   - (A) stripe
   - (B) strain
   - (C) string
   - (D) struck
   - (E) strike
   - (F) NONE

4. Rosa _____ the pretty blanket over the children's bed.
   - (A) sprinkle
   - (B) sprain
   - (C) sprout
   - (D) spring
   - (E) spread
   - (F) NONE

5. We had _____ for dinner last night.
   - (A) shriek
   - (B) shrub
   - (C) shrink
   - (D) shred
   - (E) shrimp
   - (F) NONE

6. The doctor gave Pat medicine for her sore _____.
   - (A) thread
   - (B) throw
   - (C) three
   - (D) throat
   - (E) throne
   - (F) NONE

7. The boys saw a _____ face in the kitchen window.
   - (A) strap
   - (B) strike
   - (C) stream
   - (D) strange
   - (E) stripe
   - (F) NONE

8. Susan helped Joan and Steve _____ the dirty floor.
   - (A) screen
   - (B) scraper
   - (C) scramble
   - (D) scream
   - (E) scrub
   - (F) NONE

9. When the sunlight is strong, we often have to _____.
   - (A) squash
   - (B) squeal
   - (C) square
   - (D) squint
   - (E) squeak
   - (F) NONE

10. There is a _____ of dirt on the window.
    - (A) straw
    - (B) strength
    - (C) straight
    - (D) street
    - (E) streak
    - (F) NONE

UNIT 16
Changing y to i Concepts

1. Look at the words **city, lady, puppy.** All of these words end with a **y** and have a _____ right before the letter **y.**
   (A) d   (B) vowel   (C) consonant

2. Look at the words **city** and **cities.** The word **city** ends with a **y** and has a consonant right before the **y.** In changing the word **city** to **cities,** the letter **y** was changed to an **i** before the ending _____ was added.
   (A) ed   (B) es   (C) s

3. Look at the words **lady** and **ladies.** The letter **y** was changed to an _____ before the ending **es** was added.
   (A) e   (B) l   (C) i

4. Look at the words **funny** and **funnier.** In the word **funnier** the letter _____ was changed to an **i** before the ending **er** was added.
   (A) f   (B) y   (C) u

5. Look at the words **tasty** and **tastier.** In the word **tastier** the **y** was changed to an **i** before the ending _____ was added.
   (A) er   (B) ar   (C) or

6. Look at the words **busy** and **busiest.** In the word **busiest** the **y** was changed to an **i** before the _____ was added.
   (A) ist   (B) ro   (C) est

7. Look at the words **lazy** and **laziest.** In the word **laziest** the **y** was _____ to an **i** before the ending **est** was added.
   (A) dropped   (B) changed   (C) added

8. Look at the words **happy** and **happily.** In the word **happily** the **y** was changed to an **i** before the ending _____ was added.
   (A) ly   (B) le   (C) y

9. Look at the words **heavy** and **heavily.** In the word **heavily** the **y** was changed to an _____ before the ending **ly** was added.
   (A) e   (B) ly   (C) i

10. Some words end with a **y** and have a consonant right before the **y.** The **y** is changed to an **i** before the **es, er, est,** or **ly** endings are _____ .
    (A) changed   (B) added   (C) dropped

1. The word **double** means two. When we double a letter we make _____ letters that are the same.

   (A) vowel   (B) two   (C) three

2. Look at the words **hit** and **hitting.** A second letter **t** is _____ before the ending **ing** is added.

   (A) dropped   (B) erased   (C) added

3. Look at the words **trap** and **trapper.** The letter **p** is doubled before the ending _____ is added.

   (A) er   (B) re   (C) ar

4. Look at the words **sad** and **saddest.** The letter _____ is doubled before the ending **est** is added.

   (A) d   (B) t   (C) s

5. Look at the words **hum** and **hummed.** The letter **m** is _____ before the ending **ed** is added.

   (A) erased   (B) doubled   (C) dropped

6. Look at the next-to-last letter in the words **hit, trap, sad, hum.** The next-to-last letter in each word is a _____ .

   (A) a   (B) consonant   (C) vowel

7. In each of the words **hit, trap, sad, hum** there is only _____ vowel before the last consonant.

   (A) one   (B) two   (C) three

8. In each of the words **hit, trap, sad, hum** the last letter is a _____ .

   (A) t   (B) consonant   (C) vowel

9. When there is only one vowel in a word and that vowel is followed by a consonant, the last consonant is doubled before the _____ **ing, est, ed** are added.

   (A) endings   (B) consonants   (C) vowels

10. If we added an **ing** ending to the word **run**, we would then have _____ .

    (A) runing   (B) running   (C) runnning

UNIT 18
Building Variant Sound Concepts

1. Say the words **car, come, cup.** In these words the letter **c** sounds like the letter _____.

   (A) b   (B) k   (C) s

2. Say the words **city, race, ice.** In these words the letter **c** sounds like an _____.

   (A) a   (B) s   (C) f

3. When the letter **c** sounds like an **s,** it is said to have a soft sound. When the letter **c** sounds like the letter **k,** it is said to have a hard _____.

   (A) shell   (B) sound   (C) time

4. Say the words **go, guess, got.** In these words the letter **g** sounds the way it does in the word _____. When the letter **g** makes this sound it is said to have a hard sound.

   (A) Gene   (B) gun   (C) gym

5. Say the words **Marge, orange, large.** In these words the letter **g** has a _____ sound. This is called its soft sound.

   (A) b   (B) p   (C) j

6. In the words **photo** and **telephone** the letters **ph** sound like the letter _____.

   (A) t   (B) gh   (C) f

7. The letter **s** has a number of different sounds. In the words **reason** and **music** the letter **s** sounds like _____.

   (A) sh   (B) z   (C) r

8. In the words **sugar** and **pleasure** the letter _____ sounds like an **sh** or **zh.**

   (A) g   (B) p   (C) s

9. In the words **attention** and **addition** the **tion** sounds like _____.

   (A) shun   (B) chin   (C) chan

10. In the words **orchestra** and **Christmas** the **ch** sounds like the letter _____.

    (A) f   (B) g   (C) k

UNIT 19
Building Silent Letter Concepts

1. Say each sound as you look at the letters in the word **sight**. The letters _____ are silent.

   (A) li   **(B) gh**   **(C) ht**

2. Say each sound as you look at the letters in the word **thumb.** The letter **b** is silent when it comes after an **m** at the _____ of a word.

   (A) end   **(B) top**   **(C) beginning**

3. Say each sound as you look at the letters in the word **knee.** The letter _____ is silent when it comes before the letter **n.**

   (A) i   **(B) n**   **(C) k**

4. Say each sound as you look at the letters in the word **patch.** The letter **t** is silent when it comes before _____ .

   (A) o   **(B) r**   **(C) ch**

5. Say each sound as you look at the letters in the word **rattle.** The second _____ of the twin consonants is silent.

   (A) t   **(B) l**   **(C) a**

6. Say each sound as you look at the letters in the word **wrong.** The letter _____ is silent when it comes before the letter **r.**

   (A) g   **(B) w**   **(C) r**

7. Say each sound as you look at the letters in the words **boat, beach, train.** In these words the first vowel is long and the second _____ is silent.

   (A) e   **(B) consonant**   **(C) vowel**

8. Say each sound as you look at the letters in the words **small** and **dress.** In these words you hear the first of the twin consonants at the end of the word, but not the _____ .

   (A) last   **(B) word**   **(C) sound**

9. Say each sound as you look at the letters in the word **spoke.** The letter _____ at the end of the word is silent.

   (A) s   **(B) e**   **(C) o**

10. Say each sound as you look at the letters in the words **chalk** and **could.** The letter _____ is silent in both words.

    (A) c   **(B) l**   **(C) d**

1. Mrs. Green's _____ can play the piano very well.

   (A) naughty   (B) sigh   (C) freight

   (D) daughter   (E) thigh   (F) NONE

2. Rosa's hair looks pretty because she _____ it each morning.

   (A) lamb   (B) combs   (C) crumb

   (D) climbs   (E) thumb   (F) NONE

3. When Ron feels tired he likes to _____.

   (A) clutch   (B) snatch   (C) itch

   (D) stretch   (E) catch   (F) NONE

4. We should _____ our hands before eating.

   (A) treat   (B) clean   (C) gleam

   (D) float   (E) stain   (F) NONE

5. Use that sharp _____ with care.

   (A) knight   (B) knock   (C) knee

   (D) knife   (E) know   (F) NONE

6. It's more personal to _____ a present for someone.

   (A) wrench   (B) wriggle   (C) wreck

   (D) wrap   (E) wreath   (F) NONE

7. Uncle Ted was angry when he made the car _____ at the light.

   (A) shall   (B) small   (C) stall

   (D) skill   (E) spill   (F) NONE

8. Peggy got a new pair of roller _____ for her birthday.

   (A) sweaters   (B) brakes   (C) crimes

   (D) slates   (E) skates   (F) NONE

9. I broke the piece of _____.

   (A) calm   (B) should   (C) talk

   (D) half   (E) chalk   (F) NONE

10. We built a beautiful _____ in the sand.

    (A) listen   (B) glisten   (C) often

    (D) castle   (E) rustle   (F) NONE

UNIT 21
Word Ending: ed

1. Listen to the sound of the **ed** in the words **jumped, liked, tripped.** The
   _____ sounds like a **t.**

   (A) ed   **(B) p**   **(C) m**

2. In the words **skipped, walked, talked** the ending **ed** sounds like a _____.

   (A) t   **(B) d**   **(C) l**

3. Say the words **planned, mailed, shaved.** Listen for the sound the **ed**
   makes. In these words the **ed** sounds like a _____.

   (A) t   **(B) d**   **(C) f**

4. Say the words **cried, climbed, saved.** In these words the _____ sounds
   like a **d.**

   (A) ed   **(B) p**   **(C) n**

5. Sometimes the **ed** sounds like a _____ as in the word **slapped.**

   (A) d   **(B) t**   **(C) b**

6. Sometimes the **ed** sounds like a _____ as in the word **yelled.**

   (A) f   **(B) t**   **(C) d**

7. Say the words **painted, wanted, hinted.** The root of each of these words
   ends with a _____.

   (A) t   **(B) l**   **(C) g**

8. Say the words **beaded, braided, depended.** The root of each of these
   words ends with a _____.

   (A) a   **(B) n**   **(C) d**

9. When root words end with a **t** or **d** and the ending **ed** is added to the root,
   the **ed** becomes a separate _____.

   (A) syllable   **(B) fight**   **(C) consonant**

10. You can hear a short _____ sound in the ending **ed** when it becomes a
    separate syllable.

    (A) u   **(B) a**   **(C) e**

UNIT 22
Building Syllabication Concepts

1. A syllable is a part of a word just as a room is part of a _____.
   (A) word   **(B) sound**   **(C) house**

2. The word **num ber** is broken into syllables. There is a little _____ between the syllables.
   (A) fight   **(B) space**   **(C) talk**

3. The words **sun, ban dit, po ta to,** and **tel e vi sion** all have a different number of _____.
   (A) faces   **(B) syllables**   **(C) words**

4. In the word **sun** you hear _____ vowel sound(s).
   (A) two   **(B) one**   **(C) three**

5. In the word **hid den** you hear two vowel sounds, a short **i** and a short **e.** The word **hidden** has _____ syllables.
   (A) one   **(B) two**   **(C) three**

6. In the word **cen ti pede** you hear three vowel sounds, a short **e,** a short **i,** and a long **e.** There are _____ syllables.
   (A) two   **(B) three**   **(C) four**

7. There are as many syllables in a word as there are vowels that you _____.
   (A) know   **(B) hear**   **(C) write**

8. In the word **time** you see two vowels, but you hear only _____.
   (A) three   **(B) one**   **(C) e**

9. Clap your hands as you say each syllable in the word **entertain.** You clapped _____ times.
   (A) two   **(B) three**   **(C) four**

10. Clap your hands as you say each syllable in the word **messenger.** You clapped _____ times.
    (A) three   **(B) four**   **(C) five**

1. Between which two letters is the word **per form** broken?

   (A) e and r   (B) o and r   (C) r and f

2. Between which two letters is the word **slen der** broken?

   (A) e and n   (B) n and d   (C) d and e

3. Between which two letters is the word **mer chant** broken?

   (A) r and c   (B) c and h   (C) e and r

4. The first syllable of the word **car pet** ends with the letter _____.

   (A) a   (B) r   (C) p

5. The first syllable of the word **hel met** ends with the letter _____.

   (A) m   (B) l   (C) e

6. Say the word **wil der ness.** The second syllable is _____.

   (A) dern   (B) der   (C) ness

7. Say the word **porcupine.** The second syllable is _____.

   (A) cu   (B) por   (C) pine

8. Say the word **cinnamon.** The second syllable is _____.

   (A) mon   (B) cin   (C) na

9. Say the word **introduction.** The third syllable is _____.

   (A) duc   (B) tro   (C) tion

10. Say the word **valentine.** The first syllable is _____.

    (A) val   (B) en   (C) tine

UNIT 24
Building VCC Pattern Concepts

1. In order to figure out long words, we sometimes need to break them into
   _____.

   (A) vowels   (B) consonants   (C) parts

2. Long words must be broken in certain places before we can _____ them
   out.

   (A) throw   (B) figure   (C) help

3. In order to find out where to break long words, we must find out how
   many _____ come after the first vowel.

   (A) consonants   (B) words   (C) friends

4. The first vowel in the word **whĭsper** is _____. A **V** is placed over the
   vowel. The **V** stands for vowel.

   (A) i   (B) e   (C) p

5. Right after the first vowel in the word **whĭsper** there are _____ consonants.
   A letter **C** is placed over each of them. The **C** stands for consonant.

   (A) two   (B) five   (C) six

6. In the word **whĭsper** the letter after the **p** is an **e. E** is _____ a consonant.
   Therefore, only two consonants come right after the first vowel.

   (A) not   (B) maybe   (C) always

7. In the word **music** there is only one _____ right after the first vowel.

   (A) note   (B) m   (C) consonant

8. In the word **farther** there are _____ consonants right after the first vowel.

   (A) two   (B) three   (C) four

9. The marks over **whĭsper, mŭsĭc, fãrthẽr** show us that the number of
   _____ right after the first vowel is not always the same.

   (A) sentences   (B) consonants   (C) words

10. Count the consonants right after the first vowel in **member.** There are
    _____.

    (A) two   (B) three   (C) four

Plural means "more than one." To say "more than one cat," you can use the plural form of *cat*, which, of course, is *cats*. Most words form the plural by adding s. If the word ends with an *x*, *s*, *sh*, or *ch*, add an *es* to form the plural.

Example: one church, two churches

To form the plural of many words that end with *f* or *fe*, change the *f* or *fe* to *v* before you add *es*.

Example: one leaf, ten leaves

To form the plural of words that end with a consonant and *y*, change the *y* to *i* before you add *es*.

Example: one baby, two babies

A. Exercising Your Skill

What is a picnic? The dictionary says it is an outing where food is taken along to be eaten outside. Picnics can be held outside in the yard, on an island, on a park bench, or on the beach. The place doesn't matter, just as long as you have food and the things you need to eat it with.

Pretend that you are planning a picnic for several people. Make a list of the different kinds of food you will take. List things like napkins and cups, too. Remember that the picnic is for several people, so you will need to pack more than one of many things. When you list those things, write the plural form of the word.

B. Expanding Your Skill

Compare your picnic list with your classmates' lists. Did you find something you had forgotten? Did your classmates have any other food ideas that sound good to you? Add those to your list.

Now look over your list and circle the plural forms. Did you spell them correctly? If you're not sure, look them up in the dictionary.

C. Exploring Language

You and Jeremiah and Maria went on a picnic yesterday. Everything went wrong. Now you're writing about it. Copy the paragraph below and complete it by writing a word that makes sense in each blank. If the blank has a **P**, write the plural form of the word. Check your spelling in a dictionary.

This was a picnic that was no picnic. Jeremiah packed us a ——— , __P__ , __P__ , __P__ , and a ——— . Then he left the whole ——— home, so we had nothing to eat. Instead, we went to the snack bar and bought __P__ , __P__ , and __P__ . We also bought one bag of __P__ to share. Before we finished eating, we looked up at the sky and saw that dark __P__ were covering the sun. We got on our __P__ and rode home in the rain.

D. Expressing Yourself

Choose one of these activities.

1. How good is your memory? Test it by playing "Going on a Picnic" with your classmates. Start the game by saying, "Let's go on a picnic and take along a melon." (It doesn't *have* to be a melon. It can be anything, even an ostrich.) The next player says, "Let's go on a picnic and take along a melon and lemonade." (Again, it doesn't have to be lemonade.) Each player repeats all the things that the other players have named and then adds something new to the end of the list. The list must always be repeated completely and in the correct order. See how long the list can grow before someone makes a mistake!

2. Add more to the story in Part C. What happened on the way home from the picnic? Remember, this was a day when nothing went well, so make up something else that goes wrong. If you can, give the story a funny ending.

1. Count the consonants right after the first vowel in the word **velvet.** There are _____ of them.
   (A) four   **(B) two**   **(C) three**

2. Words such as **bucket** (VCC) and **slender** (VCC) are sometimes called **VCC** words because there are two consonants right after the first _____.
   (A) vowel   **(B) consonant**   **(C) n**

3. In some words the two consonants are _____, as in the word **sputter.**
   (A) different   **(B) funny**   **(C) the same**

4. Sometimes the two _____ after the first vowel are not the same, as in the word **winter.**
   (A) words   **(B) vowels**   **(C) consonants**

5. The word **sus pect** is broken between the two _____.
   (A) vowels   **(B) consonants**   **(C) words**

6. The word **les son** is _____ between the two consonants.
   (A) hidden   **(B) broken**   **(C) found**

7. When two consonants come right after the first vowel, we usually break the word _____ those two consonants.
   (A) before   **(B) after**   **(C) between**

8. In the word **market** we break the word between the _____.
   (A) k and t   **(B) r and k**   **(C) a and r**

9. The word **cluster** is broken between the _____.
   (A) l and u   **(B) s and t**   **(C) u and s**

10. The word **harbor** is broken between the _____.
    (A) r and b   **(B) b and o**   **(C) a and r**

1. I would like a _____ with my egg.
   (A) corner (B) muffin (C) trigger
   (D) whisper (E) traffic (F) NONE

2. Ms. Simon said she would _____ a new line leader.
   (A) indent (B) appear (C) banner
   (D) appoint (E) walnut (F) NONE

3. We stored the tins of food in the _____.
   (A) sister (B) happen (C) sturdy
   (D) differ (E) pantry (F) NONE

4. When Larry is wrong he will always _____ it.
   (A) arrest (B) plenty (C) letter
   (D) carpet (E) corner (F) NONE

5. You must carry out this _____.
   (A) order (B) tender (C) herself
   (D) village (E) upper (F) NONE

6. We were able to _____ the footprints of the rabbit.
   (A) forward (B) allow (C) rescue
   (D) swallow (E) follow (F) NONE

7. The soil in the _____ is rich.
   (A) welcome (B) cotton (C) valley
   (D) curtain (E) cannon (F) NONE

8. When did the _____ fly out of the cage?
   (A) contact (B) correct (C) control
   (D) expect (E) parrot (F) NONE

9. Mother took ten dollar bills out of her _____.
   (A) window (B) penny (C) wallet
   (D) borrow (E) enter (F) NONE

10. When we finish our work we will go to the _____.
    (A) under (B) dipper (C) pillow
    (D) pepper (E) cotton (F) NONE

1. I will _____ the whole class to the party.
   - (A) common
   - (B) mistake
   - (C) button
   - (D) invite
   - (E) invent
   - (F) NONE

2. Please wait for me in the _____ of the hotel.
   - (A) holly
   - (B) helmet
   - (C) hornet
   - (D) puppet
   - (E) lobby
   - (F) NONE

3. Jenny put the _____ in back of our car.
   - (A) hidden
   - (B) luggage
   - (C) kidnap
   - (D) corner
   - (E) connect
   - (F) NONE

4. We can find the page number if we look it up in the _____.
   - (A) garden
   - (B) infant
   - (C) insect
   - (D) window
   - (E) dinner
   - (F) NONE

5. Paul hurt his _____ when he tripped and fell.
   - (A) admire
   - (B) canvas
   - (C) borrow
   - (D) enter
   - (E) blotter
   - (F) NONE

6. The dog wagged its tail when it saw its _____.
   - (A) banjo
   - (B) gallop
   - (C) lantern
   - (D) lesson
   - (E) order
   - (F) NONE

7. We read this _____ in class today.
   - (A) chapter
   - (B) hobby
   - (C) bullet
   - (D) clutter
   - (E) bandit
   - (F) NONE

8. This _____ grows in the desert.
   - (A) cartoons
   - (B) service
   - (C) border
   - (D) cactus
   - (E) buggy
   - (F) NONE

9. A _____ of fruit makes a nice gift.
   - (A) turkey
   - (B) cannon
   - (C) basket
   - (D) robber
   - (E) balloon
   - (F) NONE

10. We must _____ the garbage in our yard.
    - (A) selfish
    - (B) muddy
    - (C) Monday
    - (D) skipper
    - (E) collect
    - (F) NONE

1. Pat and Mark wanted to enter the art _____.

   (A) conduct   (B) pattern   (C) ribbon
   (D) contest   (E) pencil   (F) NONE

2. Use this _____ to find in which direction we are traveling.

   (A) lesson   (B) office   (C) effort
   (D) member   (E) compass   (F) NONE

3. Ray was _____ from class for two days because of illness.

   (A) subject   (B) correct   (C) canvas
   (D) arrow   (E) absent   (F) NONE

4. The bridge is too _____ for the truck to cross.

   (A) temper   (B) garden   (C) napkin
   (D) narrow   (E) traffic   (F) NONE

5. The chain around her neck was made of _____.

   (A) suppose   (B) silver   (C) sudden
   (D) merry   (E) mirror   (F) NONE

6. The police officer made a _____ for all cars to stop.

   (A) sermon   (B) marbles   (C) signal
   (D) cluster   (E) master   (F) NONE

7. What kind of _____ is crawling on my hand?

   (A) enter   (B) insect   (C) person
   (D) express   (E) invite   (F) NONE

8. Jeff began to sneeze when he smelled the _____.

   (A) lesson   (B) sentence   (C) marry
   (D) thunder   (E) hidden   (F) NONE

9. Place the sliced turkey on the _____.

   (A) platter   (B) custom   (C) expect
   (D) entire   (E) return   (F) NONE

10. They will not _____ us to go into the park after dark.

    (A) errand   (B) pretend   (C) allow
    (D) inside   (E) instead   (F) NONE

1. There was no smoke coming from the _____.
   - (A) barrel
   - (B) service
   - (C) admire
   - (D) current
   - (E) chimney
   - (F) NONE

2. We had to place our two dogs in a _____.
   - (A) offer
   - (B) kennel
   - (C) trumpet
   - (D) captain
   - (E) marry
   - (F) NONE

3. If we eat too much, we will not remain _____.
   - (A) sloppy
   - (B) slumber
   - (C) slender
   - (D) fluffy
   - (E) coffee
   - (F) NONE

4. Spread some _____ on the muffin.
   - (A) butter
   - (B) bandit
   - (C) dinner
   - (D) blubber
   - (E) member
   - (F) NONE

5. Andy found a real _____ at the sale in the store.
   - (A) bitter
   - (B) bargain
   - (C) until
   - (D) party
   - (E) sadden
   - (F) NONE

6. With too many in the car we cannot ride in _____.
   - (A) comfort
   - (B) complete
   - (C) forward
   - (D) infect
   - (E) attic
   - (F) NONE

7. We crossed the _____ in a sailboat.
   - (A) channel
   - (B) hello
   - (C) chapter
   - (D) porter
   - (E) suffer
   - (F) NONE

8. Our teacher said we should _____ at the start of a paragraph.
   - (A) plaster
   - (B) public
   - (C) velvet
   - (D) indent
   - (E) picnic
   - (F) NONE

9. When we eat _____ we are eating the roots of plants.
   - (A) commas
   - (B) cotton
   - (C) carrots
   - (D) number
   - (E) sudden
   - (F) NONE

10. We really _____ the author of that book.
    - (A) candy
    - (B) cactus
    - (C) umpire
    - (D) pillow
    - (E) perhaps
    - (F) NONE

UNIT 30
Building VC Pattern Concepts

1. What is the first vowel in the word **silent?**

   (A) e   (B) i   (C) o

2. In the word **si̇lent** there is a V over the _____ vowel.

   (A) **first**   (B) **second**   (C) **short**

3. In the word **si̇lent** the C over the letter _____ shows that there is only one consonant right after the first vowel.

   (A) l   (B) n   (C) vowel

4. In the word **chȯsen** there is only one consonant right after the first _____.

   (A) **vowel**   (B) **letter**   (C) **consonant**

5. Two-syllable words such as **chosen** are sometimes called _____ words since there is only one consonant after the first vowel.

   (A) **VC**   (B) **VCC**   (C) **VCCC**

6. The words **si̇ lent, clȯ ver, pȧ per** are broken between the first _____ and the consonant right after it.

   (A) **lesson**   (B) **vowel**   (C) **name**

7. The word **cra zy** is broken between the letter **a** and the letter _____.

   (A) **r**   (B) **z**   (C) **y**

8. The word **hobo** should be broken between the _____.

   (A) **o and b**   (B) **h and o**   (C) **bread**

9. Find the first vowel and count the consonants that come right after it in the word **mo ment.** The word is broken between the _____.

   (A) **n and t**   (B) **m and e**   (C) **o and m**

10. The word **soda** is broken between the _____.

   (A) **s and o**   (B) **o and d**   (C) **d and a**

1. Say the words **mo ment, fro zen, lo cate.** The first syllable ends with a
    _____ .

    (A) long e   (B) long o   (C) short a

2. Say the words **ti ger, Chi na, spi der.** Look at the last letter of the first syl-
    lable. It is a _____ .

    (A) long a   (B) short i   (C) long i

3. Say the words **la bor, fa mous, pa per.** The first syllable ends with a
    _____ .

    (A) short a   (B) long a   (C) long i

4. Say the words **mu sic, hu mans, pu pil.** The first syllable ends with a
    _____ .

    (A) short e   (B) long u   (C) long e

5. When a vowel ends the first syllable, the vowel usually has a _____ sound.

    (A) long   (B) short   (C) silent

6. In most **VC** words (**ti ger, ho tel, mu sic, pa per**) the first vowel comes at
    the _____ of the first syllable.

    (A) start   (B) middle   (C) end

7. Look at the word **clev er.** In this word the first syllable ends with a _____ .

    (A) v   (B) l   (C) r

8. The first vowel in the word **clev er** is in the middle of the first syllable.
    This _____ has a short sound.

    (A) silent   (B) consonant   (C) vowel

9. In such words as **nev er, sev en, riv er** the first vowel is short and is in the
    _____ of the first syllable.

    (A) way   (B) middle   (C) end

10. When you meet a **VC** word that you don't know, first try a long vowel
    sound. If it doesn't make sense, change it to a _____ vowel sound.

    (A) short   (B) long   (C) no

1. Who is _____ for her beautiful paintings?

   (A) broken   (B) famous   (C) fiber

   (D) final   (E) flavor   (F) NONE

2. Please hand me a sheet of _____.

   (A) pilot   (B) zero   (C) tomatoes

   (D) besides   (E) refuse   (F) NONE

3. Bill's grandfather just underwent a _____ operation.

   (A) major   (B) slogan   (C) rodeo

   (D) produce   (E) notion   (F) NONE

4. This _____ is too cold to grow oranges.

   (A) crazy   (B) climate   (C) vacant

   (D) grocer   (E) equal   (F) NONE

5. The _____ made the meat taste better.

   (A) gravy   (B) digest   (C) recess

   (D) romance   (E) spoken   (F) NONE

6. They will _____ the parade for one hour.

   (A) pretend   (B) depend   (C) below

   (D) obey   (E) delay   (F) NONE

7. Rosa was _____ to be the class president.

   (A) ocean   (B) chosen   (C) baby

   (D) over   (E) paper   (F) NONE

8. We took a walk down a _____ street.

   (A) potatoes   (B) mines   (C) pony

   (D) shady   (E) zebra   (F) NONE

9. Robert saw a _____ run down the wall.

   (A) labor   (B) spider   (C) tiny

   (D) cozy   (E) silent   (F) NONE

10. I would be happy to do a _____ for you.

    (A) favor   (B) ruby   (C) defend

    (D) human   (E) chosen   (F) NONE

1. Look at the words **fum ble, pud dle, star tle.** There are _____ letters in the last syllable of each word.

   (A) one **(B) three** **(C) two**

2. Such words as **crum ble, sta ble, driz zle** are called "**le**" words because they end with an _____.

   (A) sle **(B) t** **(C) le**

3. Say the last syllables of the words **pad dle, lit tle, pur ple.** The "**le**" in the last syllable sounds like _____.

   (A) et **(B) all** **(C) ull as in** *pull*

4. In the words **han dle, bun dle, can dle,** the last syllables begin with a _____.

   (A) d **(B) b** **(C) l**

5. Say the words **simple, sample, pimple.** The last syllables begin with a _____.

   (A) p **(B) b** **(C) l**

6. Say the words **cattle, battle, title.** The last syllables all start with a _____.

   (A) b **(B) t** **(C) l**

7. Say the words **gargle, gurgle, juggle.** The last syllables all start with a _____.

   (A) c **(B) g** **(C) l**

8. Look at the twin consonants before the "**le**" in the word **puz zle.** They look _____.

   (A) alike **(B) different** **(C) ugly**

9. Say the word **puz zle.** You can hear the first **z,** but the _____ **z** is silent.

   (A) third **(B) first** **(C) second**

10. When there are twin consonants before the "**le**," you hear the first consonant. The second is _____.

    (A) silent **(B) short** **(C) long**

1. We saw the ducks ———— across the road.
   - (A) needle
   - (B) trample
   - (C) sickle
   - (D) battle
   - (E) waddle
   - (F) NONE

2. Do you use a ———— when you sew?
   - (A) pimple
   - (B) thimble
   - (C) gargle
   - (D) noodle
   - (E) muzzle
   - (F) NONE

3. You must not ———— yourself with my problems.
   - (A) grumble
   - (B) spindle
   - (C) muscle
   - (D) struggle
   - (E) trouble
   - (F) NONE

4. The rabbit wanted to ———— on the carrots in my garden.
   - (A) nibble
   - (B) purple
   - (C) riddle
   - (D) scribble
   - (E) juggle
   - (F) NONE

5. Automobile accidents ———— many people each year.
   - (A) rumble
   - (B) shuffle
   - (C) fumble
   - (D) strangle
   - (E) cripple
   - (F) NONE

6. Juan got a silver ———— for his new belt.
   - (A) buckle
   - (B) huddle
   - (C) tangle
   - (D) bundle
   - (E) startle
   - (F) NONE

7. I have to remove a ———— from my shoe.
   - (A) cattle
   - (B) pebble
   - (C) speckle
   - (D) paddle
   - (E) tremble
   - (F) NONE

8. Jenny's little sister has many ———— on her face.
   - (A) candle
   - (B) handles
   - (C) wrestle
   - (D) startle
   - (E) freckles
   - (F) NONE

9. We like to ———— under the covers in cold weather.
   - (A) simple
   - (B) axle
   - (C) snuggle
   - (D) snuffle
   - (E) baffle
   - (F) NONE

10. What do you feed your pet ————?
    - (A) nestle
    - (B) castle
    - (C) simple
    - (D) table
    - (E) turtle
    - (F) NONE

1. The main part of a word is called the root. Other _____ are added to it.

   (A) sentences   (B) parts   (C) words

2. The root of the word **replant** is _____. **Re** is a word part put in front of it.

   (A) plant   (B) re   (C) suffix

3. The part added to the front of a root word is called a prefix. The prefix of the word **unopened** is _____.

   (A) root   (B) un   (C) open

4. Prefixes have meanings of their own. They change the meaning of the root word. _____ means not opened.

   (A) Opened   (B) Unopened   (C) Silent

5. **Un**fair means not fair. **Un**ripe means not ripe. **Un**lock means the opposite of the root word _____.

   (A) open   (B) lock   (C) door

6. The prefix _____ at the beginning of a word often means **not** or the opposite of the root word.

   (A) un   (B) ex   (C) re

7. **Un**able, for example, means _____ able. **Un**tie, for example, means the opposite of tie.

   (A) not   (B) completely   (C) somewhat

8. **Dis**connect means the opposite of the root word _____.

   (A) friends   (B) dislike   (C) connect

9. The prefix _____ at the beginning of the word **dis**agree means the opposite of the root word agree.

   (A) com   (B) re   (C) dis

10. **Dis**honest means the _____ of the word honest.

    (A) same as   (B) bank   (C) opposite

UNIT 36
Building Prefix Concepts

1. **In**correct means not correct. **In**complete means not _____.

   (A) compare   (B) complete   (C) comfort

2. The prefix _____ added to the beginning of a word often means not or the opposite of the root word.

   (A) en   (B) in   (C) ex

3. **Im**proper means not _____.

   (A) proper   (B) sad   (C) seen

4. **Im**possible means not possible. **Im**movable means _____ movable.

   (A) all   (B) not   (C) somewhat

5. The prefix _____ added to the beginning of a word means not.

   (A) de   (B) con   (C) im

6. **Im**pure, for example, means _____ pure.

   (A) a little   (B) very   (C) not

7. **Re**build means to _____ again. **Re**paint means to paint again.

   (A) build   (B) walk   (C) write

8. The prefix _____ added to the beginning of a word means to do again.

   (A) in   (B) re   (C) dis

9. **Re**read, for example, means to read _____.

   (A) poorly   (B) again   (C) work

10. In many words the prefixes **in, im, dis** mean _____ or the opposite of the root word.

    (A) yes   (B) again   (C) not

1. Can you _____ this soup for dinner?
   - (A) rejoin
   - (B) reprint
   - (C) reheat
   - (D) retrace
   - (E) repaid
   - (F) NONE

2. We will _____ the street in honor of the President.
   - (A) reorder
   - (B) return
   - (C) rename
   - (D) remove
   - (E) regain
   - (F) NONE

3. The sheet of glass looked almost _____.
   - (A) inaccurate
   - (B) inexpensive
   - (C) inartistic
   - (D) invisible
   - (E) inactive
   - (F) NONE

4. Answers that are not right are said to be _____.
   - (A) indirect
   - (B) incorrect
   - (C) incurable
   - (D) insane
   - (E) inexperience
   - (F) NONE

5. I will not believe that my friend was _____.
   - (A) dislike
   - (B) disown
   - (C) disloyal
   - (D) disorder
   - (E) disprove
   - (F) NONE

6. Rosa saw the sun _____ behind the distant mountains.
   - (A) discolor
   - (B) disallow
   - (C) disappear
   - (D) displease
   - (E) disarm
   - (F) NONE

7. That heavy chest is _____.
   - (A) improper
   - (B) impolite
   - (C) impersonal
   - (D) immovable
   - (E) impatient
   - (F) NONE

8. It will be _____ for me to come with you now.
   - (A) impure
   - (B) impatient
   - (C) immovable
   - (D) impossible
   - (E) imperfect
   - (F) NONE

9. It is _____ to cross the street without looking both ways.
   - (A) unjust
   - (B) unwise
   - (C) unclean
   - (D) uneasy
   - (E) untested
   - (F) NONE

10. When we arrived we had to _____ all of our belongings.
    - (A) untold
    - (B) untried
    - (C) unpack
    - (D) unreal
    - (E) uneven
    - (F) NONE

1. A suffix is a word part added to the end of a _____.
   (A) story   (B) sentence   (C) word

2. In the word **mouthful** the suffix is _____.
   (A) ful   (B) less   (C) ish

3. In the word **homeless** the suffix is _____.
   (A) care   (B) less   (C) missing

4. **Less, ful, er, est, ish, ness, ly, ment, able, tion** are some of the _____ added to words.
   (A) roots   (B) prefixes   (C) suffixes

5. Brown**ish** means somewhat brown. Child**ish** means like that of a child. Cloud**y** means having clouds. Salt**y** means having _____.
   (A) soap   (B) rain   (C) salt

6. The examples in the sentence above show us that the suffix _____ or **y** at the end of a word means somewhat or like or having.
   (A) o   (B) ish   (C) ment

7. Clown**ish,** for example, means like that of a clown. Bump**y**, for example, means having _____.
   (A) manners   (B) friends   (C) bumps

8. Sick**ness** means the state or condition of being sick. Polite**ness** means the state or condition of being _____.
   (A) rude   (B) polite   (C) impolite

9. A suffix _____ at the end of a word means a state or condition.
   (A) t   (B) ness   (C) less

10. Good**ness,** for example, means the _____ or condition of being good.
    (A) opposite   (B) prefix   (C) state

Prefixes are word parts that are added to the beginning of a word. Prefixes have their own meanings. They change the meaning of the word. The prefix *un* means "not." *Unliked* means "not liked."

A. Exercising Your Skill

Look at the prefixes below, and write each one at the top of your paper. Under each prefix, write words that begin with that prefix. Start by combining the words in the box below with one or more of the prefixes. Then think of other words to combine with each prefix. Look up all of your words in a dictionary. Are they listed? Did you spell them correctly?

dis	im	re	un
_____	_____	_____	_____
_____	_____	_____	_____
_____	_____	_____	_____
_____	_____	_____	_____

patient	obey	safe
fill	perfect	usual
place	proper	trust
honor	interesting	view

B. Expanding Your Skill

How did you do? Compare your list with your classmates' lists. Then use a dictionary to find other words that begin with those prefixes. Write the new words you find. Try switching the prefixes around. Find some words like *undo* and *redo* that combine the same root word with different prefixes. Notice how the prefixes *un* and *re* change the meaning of the root word, *do*.

C. Exploring Language

Read the story below. As you read, look carefully at the numbered words in darker type. Number a sheet of paper 1-10. On your paper, write each word beside its number. Circle the prefix. Then write the meaning of the prefix to show how it changes the meaning of the root word.

How well does your body's clock work? Do you wake up without an alarm clock, or do you need to (1) **reset** the alarm clock every night? Do you jump out of bed, or does someone have to (2) **reawaken** you several times? Do you get hungry right at noon, or does your stomach sometimes (3) **disagree** with the clock?

It's not (4) **unusual** to wake up at seven every morning. It's not at all rare to get hungry at the same time every day. Our days are, after all, the same length. A wristwatch may be fast or slow, but the hours in a day remain (5) **unchanged**.

Two men once tried to change to a twenty-eight hour day. They moved into a cave in the Kentucky mountains. The cave was dark. They saw no other people. They slept for nine hours and stayed awake for nineteen hours. One man had little trouble making the change. Within a few days, the new schedule did not seem at all (6) **disorderly** to him. For the other man, the change was (7) **impossible**. He was (8) **unable** to sleep at "night" and was tired and (9) **uneasy** during the "day." His body clock just didn't want to be (10) **rearranged**. How would yours do?

D. Expressing Yourself

What do you know about your body clock? Make a chart. Keep track of what time you go to bed and when you get up. Write down when you eat meals. Keep records for at least a week. Are the times always the same? How much do they change from day to day? Write a report about your body clock. In your report, try to use words with prefixes.

1. Cheer**ful** means full of cheer. Play**ful** means full of _____.

   (A) beans   (B) play   (C) trucks

2. The suffix _____ at the end of a word means to be full of that quality.

   (A) ment   (B) less   (C) ful

3. Truth**ful,** for example, means _____ truth.

   (A) without   (B) full of   (C) loud

4. Hope**less** means without _____. Tooth**less** means without teeth.

   (A) hope   (B) failing   (C) hop

5. The suffix _____ at the end of a word means without.

   (A) less   (B) ful   (C) space

6. Money**less,** for example, means _____ money.

   (A) quick   (B) tail   (C) without

7. The suffixes **ful** and **less** have opposite meanings. The **less** means without. The **ful** means _____.

   (A) full of   (B) none of   (C) a little of

8. Quick means fast. Quick**est** means _____ of all.

   (A) slowest   (B) newest   (C) fastest

9. The suffix _____ at the end of a word means the most or to the highest degree.

   (A) er   (B) y   (C) est

10. Bright means to give light. Bright**est** means giving the _____ light.

    (A) most   (B) least   (C) green

1. Suddenly means in a sudden manner. Quietly means in a _____ manner or way.

   (A) sleepy   (B) sad   (C) quiet

2. The suffix _____ at the end of a word means the way or manner in which something is done.

   (A) less   (B) er   (C) ly

3. Sadly, for example, means in a sad _____.

   (A) day   (B) picture   (C) way

4. Taller means more tall. Closer means more _____.

   (A) money   (B) class   (C) close

5. Some _____ have more than one meaning.

   (A) suffixes   (B) consonants   (C) periods

6. Faster, for example, means _____ fast.

   (A) very   (B) more   (C) less

7. A pitcher is one who pitches. A _____ is one who types.

   (A) type   (B) top   (C) typist

8. The suffix er or _____ at the end of a word often means something or someone.

   (A) en   (B) ist   (C) ly

9. A worker, for example, means a person who works. A violinist, for example, is a _____ who plays the violin.

   (A) thing   (B) person   (C) machine

10. The suffix er means more. It also means something or _____ depending on how it is used.

    (A) someone   (B) birds   (C) watery

1. Addi**tion** means the act of adding. Collec**tion** means the _____ of collecting.
   (A) act   **(B) nothing**   **(C) money**

2. The suffix _____ at the end of a word means the act, condition, or state of being.
   (A) ly   **(B) less**   **(C) tion**

3. Elec**tion,** for example, means the _____ of electing.
   (A) vote   **(B) act**   **(C) fun**

4. Wash**able** means that which can be washed. _____ means that which can work.
   (A) Marble   **(B) Laughable**   **(C) Workable**

5. The suffix _____ at the end of a word means that which can do something or is suitable for something.
   (A) est   **(B) ent**   **(C) able**

6. Drink**able,** for example, means something that _____ drunk.
   (A) must be   **(B) cannot be**   **(C) can be**

7. Enjoy**ment** means the act, state, or condition of enjoying. Govern**ment** is the _____ of governing or that which governs.
   (A) end   **(B) start**   **(C) act**

8. The suffix _____ at the end of a word means an act, state, or condition.
   (A) ful   **(B) ish**   **(C) ment**

9. Agree**ment,** for example, means the act or state of _____.
   (A) friendship   **(B) agreeing**   **(C) mind**

10. The _____ **ment** and **tion** both show a condition or act or state of being.
    (A) suffixes   **(B) prefixes**   **(C) roots**

1. I enjoy watching _____ dancers on the stage.

   (A) graceful   (B) healthful   (C) fearful

   (D) wasteful   (E) painful   (F) NONE

2. A famous and _____ painting was stolen from the museum.

   (A) tireless   (B) needless   (C) priceless

   (D) seedless   (E) cheerless   (F) NONE

3. The truck's engine is very _____.

   (A) faithful   (B) powerful   (C) careful

   (D) delightful   (E) cheerful   (F) NONE

4. I am very tired because I had a _____ night.

   (A) sleepless   (B) fatness   (C) bottomless

   (D) coldness   (E) powerless   (F) NONE

5. Just one copy of the book was _____ at the store.

   (A) trainable   (B) excusable   (C) honorable

   (D) likable   (E) available   (F) NONE

6. I hope my sweater is _____.

   (A) washable   (B) enjoyable   (C) workable

   (D) movable   (E) sayable   (F) NONE

7. Margaret isn't likely to get over her _____ without medicine.

   (A) plainness   (B) illness   (C) readiness

   (D) likeness   (E) brightness   (F) NONE

8. The _____ in the basement is worse.

   (A) politeness   (B) quietness   (C) foolishness

   (D) thickness   (E) dampness   (F) NONE

9. We will study about the _____ of our country.

   (A) amusement   (B) appointment   (C) payment

   (D) argument   (E) government   (F) NONE

10. Juan said his family was planning to move to a new _____.

    (A) apartment   (B) punishment   (C) statement

    (D) shipment   (E) treatment   (F) NONE

1. This morning Pat brought her stamp ——— to school.
   (A) education   (B) collection   (C) location
   (D) election   (E) direction   (F) NONE

2. Steve would do much better in school if he paid ———.
   (A) description   (B) preparation   (C) location
   (D) correction   (E) attention   (F) NONE

3. The clay cliffs had a ——— color at sunset.
   (A) reddish   (B) ticklish   (C) devilish
   (D) boyish   (E) bookish   (F) NONE

4. I was sent home because I felt ———.
   (A) selfish   (B) feverish   (C) foolish
   (D) accomplish   (E) babyish   (F) NONE

5. The ——— of our school band led us onto the field.
   (A) wrongdoer   (B) director   (C) selector
   (D) traveler   (E) explorer   (F) NONE

6. Rosa handles the paintbrush with the skill of an ———.
   (A) duelist   (B) chemist   (C) artist
   (D) scientist   (E) druggist   (F) NONE

7. That was the ——— meal that I ever had eaten.
   (A) dewiest   (B) smokiest   (C) tastiest
   (D) rustiest   (E) floweriest   (F) NONE

8. It was the ——— sky I ever had seen.
   (A) happiest   (B) starriest   (C) shakiest
   (D) laziest   (E) hungriest   (F) NONE

9. We were very ——— after working in the garden.
   (A) bravery   (B) honesty   (C) cruelty
   (D) thirsty   (E) poetry   (F) NONE

10. This rug is ——— nine feet long.
    (A) nervously   (B) eagerly   (C) famously
    (D) nearly   (E) angrily   (F) NONE

1. In words of two or more syllables, one of the syllables is spoken with more force than the _____.
    (A) radio   **(B) other(s)**   **(C) past**

2. The _____ that is spoken the loudest is said to be accented.
    (A) story   **(B) syllable**   **(C) silence**

3. The accent mark is placed just after the _____ that is said the loudest.
    (A) syllable   **(B) word**   **(C) sentence**

4. In the word **de part´ ment** the second syllable is accented. The accent mark comes right _____ that syllable.
    (A) before   **(B) after**   **(C) away**

5. The _____ syllable of the word **ti ger** is accented.
    (A) first   **(B) second**   **(C) third**

6. In some of these exercises the accented syllable will be in _____ letters as in the word **ho TEL.**
    (A) capital   **(B) little**   **(C) missing**

7. One look at the word **BA by** tells you that the _____ syllable is accented.
    (A) first   **(B) last**   **(C) third**

8. Say the accented syllable loudly. Whisper the unaccented syllable. This will help you hear the _____.
    (A) difference   **(B) call**   **(C) radio**

9. In the word **COW hand** say **cow** loudly. Whisper the _____.
    (A) news   **(B) hand**   **(C) horse**

10. In the word **de PART ment** you whisper the first and the last syllables. You say _____ loudly.
    (A) part   **(B) de**   **(C) ment**

1. Among the words you will find **NEED less, re WRITES** and **HELP ful**, are roots, prefixes, and _____.

   (A) suffixes   (B) long o's   (C) silent f's

2. Look at the accented syllables in the words in question one. The accented syllables are in capital letters. You can see that the **less, re,** and **ful** are _____ accented.

   (A) always   (B) slightly   (C) not

3. In the words **LOVE ly, re READ, PAVE ment** the _____ get the accent.

   (A) prefixes   (B) suffixes   (C) roots

4. The last two letters in the words **BOT tle, STUM ble, TEM ple** are all _____.

   (A) le   (B) fe   (C) ne

5. Look at the accented syllable in the words **TA ble, PIM ple,** and **CAT tle.** The _____ syllable gets the accent.

   (A) first   (B) last   (C) letter

6. Say the words **com PLETE, TI ger, es CAPE.** All have a syllable with a long _____ sound.

   (A) vowel   (B) consonant   (C) music

7. In the word **com PLETE** there is a long **e** sound. In the word **TI ger** there is a long **i** sound. In the word **es CAPE** there is a _____ sound.

   (A) short i   (B) long a   (C) short a

8. In the word **ZE bra** there is a long **e** sound. In the word **SI lent** there is a long **i** sound. In the word **CHI na** there is a _____ sound.

   (A) short i   (B) long i   (C) long a

9. The syllable with the long vowel sound is the syllable that is _____.

   (A) silent   (B) accented   (C) not accented

10. In the words **SEA son** and **sup POSE** listen for the long vowel sound. The syllable with the _____ vowel sound is the one you will accent.

    (A) missing   (B) different   (C) long

UNIT 46
Building Accent Concepts

1. Try accenting each syllable in the word **po ta to.** By shifting the accent from one syllable to another, you can hear which one sounds _____.
   (A) **right**   (B) **left**   (C) **tired**

2. Try accenting the word **re mem ber** three ways: **RE mem ber, re MEM ber, re mem BER.** The second syllable should be _____.
   (A) **silent**   (B) **whispered**   (C) **accented**

3. Accent the word **ti ger** on each syllable. Try saying **TI ger,** then **ti GER.** When you accent the _____ syllable it sounds right.
   (A) **first**   (B) **second**   (C) **neither**

4. Tap your desk as you say the word **el e phant.** When you say the accented syllable, tap the desk with more force than when you say the _____ one.
   (A) **unaccented**   (B) **nearest**   (C) **middle**

5. Say the words **MO ment, LA dy, PI lot.** All are accented on the _____ syllable.
   (A) **first**   (B) **second**   (C) **third**

6. Say the words **ex CUSE, com PLETE, un LOCK.** All are accented on the _____ syllable.
   (A) **first**   (B) **second**   (C) **third**

7. Say the words **lo CA tion, at TEN tion, un LOCK ing.** All are accented on the _____ syllable.
   (A) **second**   (B) **first**   (C) **third**

8. Say the words **TEL e phone, AR gu ment, DIF fer ent.** All are accented on the _____ syllable.
   (A) **first**   (B) **second**   (C) **third**

9. Say the words **dic tion ar y, tel e vi sion.** Both are accented on the _____ syllable.
   (A) **first**   (B) **third**   (C) **last**

10. Say the words **pot, cane, run.** There isn't any _____ since there is only one syllable in each word.
    (A) **word**   (B) **accent**   (C) **syllable**

1. Does this game come with _____?
   (A) instructions   (B) advertise   (C) conventions
   (D) kindergartens   (E) continents   (F) NONE

2. What crops are grown on the _____?
   (A) convince   (B) suddenly   (C) publisher
   (D) plantation   (E) constructed   (F) NONE

3. The _____ of the building is made of concrete.
   (A) alphabet   (B) elementary   (C) foundation
   (D) surprising   (E) terrible   (F) NONE

4. John did not _____ my telephone number.
   (A) northerly   (B) property   (C) belonged
   (D) escaping   (E) remember   (F) NONE

5. There were ten people _____ on board ship.
   (A) properly   (B) benefit   (C) remaining
   (D) splendidly   (E) cemetery   (F) NONE

6. Our teacher taught us how to _____ long numbers.
   (A) interest   (B) punishment   (C) possible
   (D) volcano   (E) multiply   (F) NONE

7. We gave our tickets to the _____ on the train.
   (A) appearing   (B) conductor   (C) victory
   (D) extremely   (E) syllable   (F) NONE

8. When did the birds _____ from the area?
   (A) military   (B) infection   (C) disappear
   (D) connecting   (E) deliver   (F) NONE

9. I had a long _____ with my aunt on the phone.
   (A) surrounding   (B) magnify   (C) conversation
   (D) deciding   (E) subject   (F) NONE

10. A _____ can squeeze through a tiny opening.
    (A) succeeded   (B) organize   (C) factory
    (D) discover   (E) promotion   (F) NONE

1. In time of an _____ people should remain calm.
   - (A) attention
   - (B) minister
   - (C) emergency
   - (D) education
   - (E) tomahawk
   - (F) NONE

2. Ms. Bellwood wasn't _____ with Jenny's answer.
   - (A) intelligent
   - (B) porcupine
   - (C) identity
   - (D) satisfied
   - (E) criminal
   - (F) NONE

3. The _____ talked about the trip to the New World.
   - (A) develop
   - (B) deliver
   - (C) professor
   - (D) colorful
   - (E) kangaroo
   - (F) NONE

4. I hope you will feel _____ in this chair.
   - (A) condition
   - (B) electric
   - (C) comfortable
   - (D) beautiful
   - (E) confusion
   - (F) NONE

5. The chief had to _____ the cause of the fire.
   - (A) investigate
   - (B) elected
   - (C) famously
   - (D) example
   - (E) surrounded
   - (F) NONE

6. Juan found his father's old army _____ in the attic.
   - (A) unselfish
   - (B) develop
   - (C) hurricane
   - (D) uniform
   - (E) motorist
   - (F) NONE

7. Who is the _____ of this hotel?
   - (A) manager
   - (B) dinosaur
   - (C) musical
   - (D) lemonade
   - (E) telephone
   - (F) NONE

8. Ms. Willis asked for everyone's _____.
   - (A) imagine
   - (B) examine
   - (C) pretended
   - (D) opposite
   - (E) attention
   - (F) NONE

9. The store owner sold a hat to the _____.
   - (A) selecting
   - (B) customer
   - (C) marvelous
   - (D) membership
   - (E) protected
   - (F) NONE

10. Did you see those photos in the _____?
    - (A) permission
    - (B) popular
    - (C) explosion
    - (D) magazine
    - (E) correctly
    - (F) NONE

1. The letter was delivered by a _____.

   (A) messenger   (B) reliable   (C) suggestion
   (D) opinion   (E) structure   (F) NONE

2. Kerry sat in the _____ for the movie.

   (A) suitable   (B) satisfy   (C) balcony
   (D) potato   (E) direction   (F) NONE

3. The _____ have just boarded the ship.

   (A) passengers   (B) entertain   (C) inventions
   (D) enormous   (E) opportunity   (F) NONE

4. The pool water was just the right _____ for a late afternoon swim.

   (A) accidents   (B) inspectors   (C) harmonize
   (D) temperature   (E) intended   (F) NONE

5. She _____ that I try some of her soup.

   (A) insisted   (B) athletic   (C) entertain
   (D) expression   (E) offering   (F) NONE

6. Maria received an award for perfect _____ during the school year.

   (A) collected   (B) perfection   (C) traveler
   (D) attendance   (E) contented   (F) NONE

7. I had a _____ with cheese for lunch today.

   (A) collection   (B) hamburger   (C) tornado
   (D) entering   (E) statement   (F) NONE

8. Let's not get into an _____ over the answer to his question.

   (A) umbrella   (B) argument   (C) liberty
   (D) condition   (E) innocent   (F) NONE

9. I need your _____ on this letter before it can be mailed.

   (A) signature   (B) ignorant   (C) paratrooper
   (D) probably   (E) dandelion   (F) NONE

10. We have to take the _____ up to the tenth floor.

    (A) wonderful   (B) company   (C) advantage
    (D) elevator   (E) opening   (F) NONE

1. Barbara's mother gave her _____ to go on the trip.
   (A) necessary   (B) finally   (C) terribly
   (D) separate   (E) permission   (F) NONE

2. Rob asked me to _____ him to my parents.
   (A) introduce   (B) ornament   (C) operation
   (D) ambulance   (E) property   (F) NONE

3. This _____ I am taking my sister to the zoo.
   (A) medicine   (B) afternoon   (C) peppermint
   (D) permission   (E) introduce   (F) NONE

4. The teacher asked us which _____ from the book was our favorite.
   (A) recently   (B) enjoyment   (C) department
   (D) character   (E) boundary   (F) NONE

5. That building has a _____ view of the ocean.
   (A) apartment   (B) engineer   (C) activity
   (D) delightful   (E) principal   (F) NONE

6. San used a _____ to find the meaning of the word.
   (A) dictionary   (B) dangerous   (C) parakeet
   (D) assistant   (E) shrubbery   (F) NONE

7. A _____ swing helps a baseball player hit many home runs.
   (A) formation   (B) powerful   (C) alligator
   (D) thoughtfulness   (E) propeller   (F) NONE

8. Kelly called the restaurant to make an eight o'clock _____ for dinner.
   (A) expensive   (B) disappear   (C) reservation
   (D) president   (E) vegetables   (F) NONE

9. Judy played the _____ in the school band.
   (A) champion   (B) preparing   (C) refreshment
   (D) attending   (E) remember   (F) NONE

10. Tom made a sandwich with cheese, lettuce, and _____.
    (A) monument   (B) instantly   (C) mystery
    (D) tomatoes   (E) violins   (F) NONE

Some words have more than one syllable. When you say the word, you say one of the syllables with extra force. That extra force is called an accent. In a dictionary, an accent mark (´) is placed just after the syllable that is accented. For instance, in a dictionary, you will find the word *accent* written like this: ac´cent. The accent mark comes after the first syllable of the word *accent* because the first syllable is said with extra force. Which syllable is accented in the word *syllable*?

A. Exercising Your Skill

When you read a new word, you may not know which syllable is accented. You can't tell by the spelling. If you want to find out how to say the word properly, do some simple detective work. Ask someone who knows, or look in a dictionary.

There is no mystery to syllables and accents, but the words in the box below are all good words for a mystery story. Do you know how to accent them, or will you have to do some detective work? Make three columns on your paper. Label them 1, 2, and 3. Say each word in the box. Under number 1, write all the words from the box that have the accent on the first syllable. Under numbers 2 and 3, write the words that have the accent on the second or third syllable.

detective	watchful	explanation
secret	adventure	whisper
sneaker	remember	accidentally
puzzle	surprise	discover

What other mystery words do you know? Add them to the proper columns.

B. Expanding Your Skill

For how many mystery words have you "detected" the accents? Try writing those words in syllables and adding the accent mark. Place the accent mark after the syllable that is said with the most force. Use a dictionary to check your work.

C. Exploring Language

It's a mystery, all right. A "ghost writer" has written the story below but has left out the key words. What really happens in the story? Read it through. Then rewrite it on a sheet of paper. Use your own words in the spaces.

Up, Up, and Away

The _____ looked down at the _____ . He got out his _____ and looked at the _____ again. He couldn't figure it out. The _____ started over there by the _____ . Right here they _____ . Where did they go?

He called to his _____ , Rosa. "What do you think?" he asked her.

Rosa looked around. She looked up at the _____ . "I know what happened," she said. "They tip-toed along here and waited here for a _____ . It carried them away. You'll find them all up there in the _____ ."

D. Expressing Yourself

Real life mysteries happen every day. They happen to you, don't they?

You haven't seen your cat all morning. Suddenly she's right there, sitting beside you. How did she get there?

You put your favorite pencil on the bookcase. It disappears. A month later you find it under your bed. How did it get there? Write about one of your mysteries, or, if you prefer, write about something that just seems strange to you.

CONCEPTS DEVELOPED

UNIT

1. BUILDING VOWEL CONCEPTS
2. BUILDING VOWEL CONCEPTS
3. BUILDING VOWEL CONCEPTS
4. CHOOSING VOWEL SOUNDS
5. CHOOSING VOWEL SOUNDS
6. CHOOSING VOWEL SOUNDS
7. COMPOUND WORD PRACTICE
8. COMPOUND WORD PRACTICE
9. COMPOUND WORD PRACTICE
10. DIPHTHONG CONCEPTS & PRACTICE
11. DIPHTHONG CONCEPTS & PRACTICE
12. AR, OR PATTERN PRACTICE
13. ER, IR, UR PATTERN PRACTICE
14. PLURAL CONCEPTS
15. TRIPLE LETTER PRACTICE
16. CHANGING Y TO I CONCEPTS
17. DOUBLING LAST LETTER CONCEPTS
18. BUILDING VARIANT SOUND CONCEPTS
19. BUILDING SILENT LETTER CONCEPTS
20. SILENT LETTER PRACTICE
21. WORD ENDING: ED
22. BUILDING SYLLABICATION CONCEPTS
23. BUILDING SYLLABICATION CONCEPTS
24. BUILDING VCC PATTERN CONCEPTS
25. BUILDING VCC PATTERN CONCEPTS

UNIT

26. VCC PATTERN PRACTICE
27. VCC PATTERN PRACTICE
28. VCC PATTERN PRACTICE
29. VCC PATTERN PRACTICE
30. BUILDING VC PATTERN CONCEPTS
31. BUILDING VC PATTERN CONCEPTS
32. VC PATTERN PRACTICE
33. LE PATTERN CONCEPTS
34. LE PATTERN PRACTICE
35. BUILDING PREFIX CONCEPTS
36. BUILDING PREFIX CONCEPTS
37. PREFIX PATTERN PRACTICE
38. BUILDING SUFFIX CONCEPTS
39. BUILDING SUFFIX CONCEPTS
40. BUILDING SUFFIX CONCEPTS
41. BUILDING SUFFIX CONCEPTS
42. SUFFIX PATTERN PRACTICE
43. SUFFIX PATTERN PRACTICE
44. BUILDING ACCENT CONCEPTS
45. BUILDING ACCENT CONCEPTS
46. BUILDING ACCENT CONCEPTS
47. UNLOCKING LONGER WORDS
48. UNLOCKING LONGER WORDS
49. UNLOCKING LONGER WORDS
50. UNLOCKING LONGER WORDS